Arif Goes Shopping

by Charlotte al-Qadi

illustrated by Rupert Van Wyk

CAMBRIDGE
UNIVERSITY PRESS

UCL
Institute of Education

Mum puts apples
in the trolley.

Mum puts oranges
in the trolley.

Mum puts milk
in the trolley.

Mum puts juice
in the trolley.

9

Mum puts rice
in the trolley.

Mum puts pizza
in the trolley.

Mum puts me
in the trolley!

Arif Goes Shopping ☙ Charlotte al-Qadi

Teaching notes written by Sue Bodman and Glen Franklin

Using this book

Developing reading comprehension

This engaging tale of what happens when Mum and Arif go shopping is told through a simple repetitive sentence structure. The text tells us what Mum selects from the shelves, but the real story is about Arif, as the title tells us. He enthusiastically helps Mum select the items and put them in the trolley. But shopping is hard work and soon it is a very tired Arif being placed in the trolley.

Grammar and sentence structure

- Text is well-spaced to support the development of one-to-one correspondence.
- Two lines of text on each page support the reinforcement of return sweep whilst tracking a slightly longer text.
- In contexts where children are learning English as an additional language, support by rehearsing the sentence structure orally before introducing the book.

Word meaning and spelling

- Check vocabulary predictions by attending to the first letter of nouns ('apples', 'oranges', 'milk', 'juice', 'rice', 'pizza').
- Reinforce recognition of frequently occurring words ('Mum' 'in' 'the' 'puts').

Curriculum links

Maths – How much did each item of shopping cost? Maths investigations could calculate how much two or more ingredients cost, or work out how much change Arif could expect. Local currencies would provide the best context for this investigation.

Geography – What do we eat? Do Arif and Mum choose the same staple items as the children in your class? Or do they usually buy different things? This discussion could lead to creating block graphs to investigate which foods the children enjoy the most.

Learning Outcomes

Children can:

- understand that print carries meaning and is read from left to right, top to bottom
- use initial letter information to check understanding of picture information
- track two lines of simple repetitive text.

A guided reading lesson

Book Introduction

Give a book to each child and read the title.

Orientation

Give a brief orientation to the text: *Mum and Arif go shopping. Mum puts each item in the trolley. Arif helps Mum. Let's see if he is good at helping.*

Preparation

Page 2: *Mum puts apples in the trolley. Point to each word carefully as I read.* Read the line slowly enough for the children to match carefully as you read. Watch to make sure they control the return sweep when it happens. Support and repeat if necessary.

Say: *Well done. Make sure you point carefully when you read by yourself.*

Page 4. Say: *What does Mum put in now? You think oranges? How will we know it you're right? Let's check the word.* Demonstrate by holding your book so the children can see you track through the first line of text and pause to put your finger under the first letter of 'oranges'. Continue: *The letter helps us know that the word is 'oranges'. We have to check the first letter, 'oranges'. I can hear 'o'. I can see the letter we use to write the 'o' sound.*

Page 6: *So how can we check what Mum puts in the trolley next?* Encourage the children to demonstrate finding the word they need to think about by tracking